MYSTERIOUS MONSTERS

John Townsend

Raintree

Chicago, Illinois

For information, address the publisher:
Raintree, 100 N. LaSalle, Suite 1200, Chicago, IL 60602

Printed and bound in China
08 07 06 05 04
10 9 8 7 6 5 4 3 2 1

Library of Congress Cataloging-in-Publication Data
Townsend, John, 1955-
  Mysterious monsters / John Townsend.
      v. cm. -- (Out there?)
Includes bibliographical references (p.   ).
Contents: Monsters of myth and fiction -- Real beasts of mystery --
Mystery beasts of the mountains -- Monsters of the sky -- Monsters of
the lake -- Monsters of the seas.
  ISBN 1-4109-0564-0 (lib. bdg.), 1-4109-0965-4 (Pbk.)
  1. Monsters--Juvenile literature. [1. Monsters.] I. Title.
  QL89.T68 2004
  001.944--dc21
                        2003010544

Acknowledgments
The publisher wishes to thank the following for permission to reproduce photographs:
Pp. 4, 4–5, 6–7, 7, 8–9, 10–11, 12–13, 51 Ronald Grant Archive; pp. 6, 9, 28–29, Oxford Scientific Films;
pp. 6, 14–15, 16, 25 (left), 36, 42–43, 46, 48–49 NHPA; p. 10 Science Photo Library; p. 11 20th Century Fox
Televison/Kobal Collection; pp. 12, 50 (right) Mary Evans Picture Library; pp. 13, 26, 25 (right), 30–31, 32, 33,
 34, 35, 37, 51 Corbis; p. 15 Bob Krist/Corbis; p. 17 The Queen Victoria Museum, Tasmania/Gondwana Studios;
pp. 18–19 John Cleare Mountain Photography; pp. 19, 27, 28, 29, 38 Topham Picturepoint; pp. 20 (right), 22
(right, left), 24, 30, 31, 34–35, 43, 44–45 Fortean Picture Library; pp. 20–21 Patterson/Gimlin/Fortean Picture
Library; p. 23 Jacques Langevin/Corbis; pp. 32–33, 47 Natural History Museum; 36–37 Charlie Walker
Collection/Topham Picturepoint; pp. 38–39 Australian Museum/Nature Force; 39 Wm. Leo Smith; pp.
 40–41 Haroldo Palo Jr./NHPA; p. 42 New Zealand Herald/Corbis; p. 44 Karl Ammann/Corbis; p. 48
Galen Rowell/Corbis; p. 50 (left) Kobal Collection.

Cover photographer used with permission of Imagebank/Getty Images.

CONTENTS

Some words are shown in bold, **like this.** You can find out what they mean by looking in the glossary. You can also look out for them in the "Weird Words" box at the bottom of each page.

MONSTERS RULE!

MONSTERS GO BACK A LONG WAY

Creepy monsters have been popular throughout human history:

- Thousands of years ago, people told stories of creatures that ate us alive.
- Children's fairy tales are full of evil giants or hungry wolves.
- Movies and computer games feature battles against scary beasts.

Some of the first stories people ever told were of scary beasts. Since humans first sat around fires to tell stories, monsters have been the stuff of **folklore.**

People would tell stories of dragons breathing fire. They talked about giant human-eating birds. They drew huge **serpents** in the mud. Great **myths** grew from these weird and wonderful stories about monsters.

All around the world, people still talk about strange beasts in secret places. After all, there are many **remote** places that are perfect hiding places for monsters.

King Kong is one of the most famous movie monsters.

WEIRD WORDS   **folklore**   old beliefs, myths, and stories
myth   made-up tale, told over many years

SCARY STORIES

A giant **reptile** creeps up from the sewers. A fierce wolfman claws at the door. A huge **dinosaur** attacks the city. We still love monster movies that make us scream.

The **ancient** Greeks were just the same. They loved monster stories full of fear and danger. If the hero killed the terrible beast, people were happy because it was like good overcoming evil.

Mystery beasts make great stories. But do monsters really exist? Or are they just made up for a little excitement? Maybe some monsters are really **lurking** in secret places. Read on and make up your own mind.

FIND OUT LATER...

Are living dinosaurs still out there?

Do water dragons really hide in lakes and oceans?

What if monsters still hide in the mountains?

remote   far away from people
serpent   large snake

MONSTERS OF MYTH AND FICTION

The hippogryph makes a good taxi for Harry Potter in *The Prisoner of Azkaban.*

Monsters in the movies make money. They are good for **business** and sell millions of videos and DVDs. People in the 21st century still love weird creatures, and new ones are being created all the time. Today, with the help of special effects, teeth bite us from the screen.

It could be a troll or an orc in *The Lord of the Rings*. From *Eight-Legged Freaks* to *Shrek* to *The Incredible Hulk*—we are crazy about strange beasts. Maybe monsters help us face the real troubles in life. After we tremble at the horrors on the screen, our real-life problems do not seem so bad after all.

HIPPOGRYPH

Some beasts of **myth** are kind of a mix. The hippogryph has the hind legs of a horse, with the body and wings of a gryphon. A gryphon is part lion, part eagle. It comes from old European myths.

The Creature From The Black Lagoon is a horror movie made in 1954. This is the Gill-Man.

WEIRD WORDS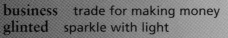

business   trade for making money
glinted   sparkle with light

HOME-MADE MONSTER

*The body lay on the table under a sheet. Lightning flashed in the night sky. Wires crackled and fizzed. Thunder cracked . . . as the brain sparked into life. Slowly the eyes opened. The sheet slid to the floor as the creature **stirred**. It sat upright on the table. A flash lit the room in a streak of silver. It **glinted** from the bolt in the monster's neck . . .*

Frankenstein is the famous story of a human monster that still scares people today. Dr. Frankenstein made his creature from dead human body parts, in the hope of creating life. When his monster attacked with superhuman strength, it was time to run . . . .

FRANKENSTEIN'S MONSTER

Mary Shelley wrote the novel *Frankenstein* in 1816. Nothing like this had been written before. In 1931 the most famous *Frankenstein* movie was made. The actor Boris Karloff played the monster.

Frankenstein, from 1931, is thought to be one of the best horror films ever made. ❯❯

WEREWOLVES

In the days when wolves hunted in most woods and hills, humans had to beware. People's fear of wolves was very real. But there were stories of something even worse: a beast that was half-human, half-wolf.

Such beliefs came from the **Dark Ages.** As soon as a full moon appeared, the werewolf would turn into a wolf-like monster and hunt for human meat. If one of these wolves bit you, you would become a werewolf, too. On the night of a full moon, you would start to change. Your teeth would get sharper. You would grow hair on your hands and face. When you saw the moon, you would throw back your head and howl.

A wolf's howl at night can send a shiver down your spine.

THE WOLF

A wolf is hardly a monster. It is very similar to a dog. Yet wild stories about this night hunter can scare us. This is the power of **fiction**.

WEIRD WORDS   Dark Ages   over 1,000 years ago, when people knew little about the world or science

ONCE BITTEN

The **legend** of humans turning into wolf-like creatures goes back hundreds of years to the forests of Europe. It may have begun with the disease **rabies.** People bitten by a wild dog with rabies would soon foam at the mouth and growl with fever. It seemed like they were turning into wild animals. There was no cure.

Stories spread about people being bitten and turning into beasts. If they became werewolves, there was nothing they could do. Each full moon they needed to kill. They would turn into savage monsters and run into the night with a thirst for human blood.

HOW TO BECOME A WEREWOLF

Many **ancient** beliefs came from Italy. You could be a werewolf if:

- *you were born on a Friday under a full moon;*
- *you slept with the full moon shining on your face;*
- *you drank water from the footprint of a savage wolf.*

Strange things happen during a full moon. **❮❮**

legend   story from long ago that may be partly true
rabies   disease caught from the bite of an infected animal

DEALING WITH VAMPIRES

According to some beliefs, if you sleep with garlic under your pillow, you will keep vampires away. But if you want to slay one, nothing less than a wooden **stake** right through the heart will work.

VAMPIRES

A **legend** said that when a werewolf died, it would return as a vampire. The two monsters went side by side in many early stories. Today, stories about vampires and the people who **slay** them often appear on television. For years, horror movies have scared millions of people with the dripping fangs of these "undead creatures."

The fear of vampires was very real a few hundred years ago. Legends of bloodsucking creatures came from all around the world. In China, vampires were said to have green or pink hair. Greek vampires had a woman's body and the tail of a winged **serpent**. The stories said that if they bit you, you would turn into a vampire forever.

Can we trust people who do not like garlic? They may be vampires! ∨∨

Dracula is the most famous vampire. ≫

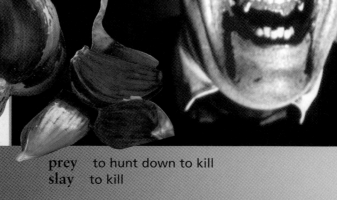

prey   to hunt down to kill
slay   to kill

DRACULA

In 1897 Bram Stoker wrote a book based on the vampire stories. Count Dracula became a modern **myth.** Modern vampire stories and movies are loosely based on Count Dracula. Most people today think of vampires as blood-drinking ex-humans. They often wear black capes, have black hair, very pale faces, and fangs. Some can turn into bats. They **prey** on human victims at night, sucking blood from the veins in their necks. They cannot stand sunlight and sleep in coffins in dark rooms underground. They have no shadows. Would you say they are monsters? You might if one was trying to feed on you!

BUFFY THE VAMPIRE SLAYER

Who would have thought vampire slaying could be a big television hit?

66

Buffy, when I said you could slay vampires and have a life, I didn't mean at the same time!

99

Giles

66

I don't like vampires. I'm going to take a stand and say they're not good.

99

Xander

Buffy has made vampire stories popular again. **‹‹**

stake   stick or post sharpened at one end

THE WORLD OF DRAGONS

GEORGE AND THE DRAGON

One hero who saved a beautiful **maiden** from a dragon's jaws was Saint George. He killed the evil dragon—a **triumph** over the powers of darkness.

Ancient stories say that if you meet a dragon, you are as good as dead. It could spit fire at you. Then it could eat you once you were cooked.

Our deep fear of being eaten alive could explain many of our monster **myths.** But dragons might be more than a myth. Perhaps there was a creature living long ago that started the stories about dragons. Otherwise, why would people from different parts of the world tell of similar beasts with **scales,** long tails, and claws? Whether they were the dragons of Greek myths or the Bible, they could be very scary. Strangely, the dragons of ancient China were believed to be friendly.

Legends say that the only way to keep a dragon away is to feed it a maiden.

WEIRD WORDS

fossils   ancient remains of animal bones and teeth
maiden   young, unmarried woman

LONG AGO

So what is a dragon like? Most stories say that a dragon:

- is like a **reptile**;
- breathes fire or poison;
- lives in or near water;
- can fly.

In many stories, it was the dragon's job to guard treasure or a special place or person. Most dragons were big and powerful. It was not wise to argue with a dragon.

So where did all these ideas come from? Could a beast like this really have lived? Did any **survive** from the age of the **dinosaurs**? Perhaps ancient people did see flying monsters. It was only in the 1800s that **fossils** proved that huge flying lizards did once exist. Maybe some still do. But today people are more likely to claim to have seen aliens than dragons.

In the latest Godzilla movie, computer animation was used to create this huge monster. ︿︿

Did fire-breathing dragons once roam the earth? ❬❬

GODZILLA

Godzilla has been a movie star for over 50 years. It keeps coming back to scare the world. The dragon-like monster was just a rubber model in the early films. But it still made some people in movie theaters faint.

scales   small, bony plates that protect the skin
triumph   success and victory

KOMODO DRAGON

You hear a sound in the grass. There is a bad smell in the air. Branches spring apart and suddenly something runs toward you. It is huge, with cold eyes and open jaws. Sharp, long teeth drip with deadly **saliva.** The monster flicks out a red tongue like a flame.

No one knew about these creatures a hundred years ago. Dragons were only supposed to be **myths.** Or they were **extinct** beasts from another age. But in 1912 a pilot crash-landed on the island of Komodo in Indonesia. He was shocked when he saw the biggest lizard in the world. At 10 feet (3 meters) long, it was one of the biggest surprises of the 20th century.

Sometimes it pays not to get too close to wildlife! ︿︿

HUMAN-EATER

In 1973 Baron Rudolph sat down to relax while his tour group went to explore Komodo. He was not seen again. A Komodo dragon ate him. All that was left was his blood-stained shirt and camera. Other tourists have since faced the same end.

Komodo dragons are very rare. There are only a few thousand left in the world. Because of this, they are now a protected **species.** ︿︿

ambush   surprise attack
boar   large wild pig

KILLERS

Komodo dragons can eat almost their own weight in meat in one meal. They wait to **ambush** their victims. These **reptiles** can run as fast as humans. They rush out from their hiding place and tear a bite from their victim. That is enough. The dragon's mouth is deadly because its teeth are full of rotting meat. This is why they smell so bad. A bite will poison the victim, who will soon die.

The Komodo dragon usually hunts wild **boar** and deer. However, it will attack, kill, and eat animal near it. This might be another Komodo dragon, or even a person. It does not seem to matter.

SIZE

A large Komodo dragon can be twice the size and weight of a human. Maybe that does not make it a real monster like the dragons of myths. But what if it had bigger members in its family? Could they still be out there somewhere?

Komodo dragons can give victims a deadly bite.

extinct   died out, never to return
saliva   mouth juices, spit

CLOSE FAMILY

The monitor lizard is the largest known lizard in Australia. It is too small to be mistaken for its "dragon" cousins. At only 6.5 feet (2 meters) long, these would hardly look like the Megalania.

This large monitor lizard eats fish and small **mammals.**

MEGALANIA

The Megalania was a real monster. Some people say it is still alive. It would probably act like a giant Komodo dragon. At up to 33 feet (10 meters) long, it would have been five times heavier than a Komodo dragon. It would be far more dangerous than today's biggest crocodile.

The mystery is whether Megalania died out in the last Ice Age 20,000 years ago. Many people say they have seen one alive in Australia's **outback.** Some have found footprints in the mud. They believe this is **evidence** the **reptile** still exists. But the footprints could be from a very large Komodo dragon, alive and well in the outback. If it is a Megalania, people had better watch out.

Part of a Megalania skeleton has been made up from **fossils** found at sites across Australia. The beasts would look a little like this.

evidence   information that can help prove if something is true or false

SIGHTINGS

Many years ago, an Australian farmer saw a huge lizard moving along the edge of his field. Using a set of fence posts, he figured out the animal's length. It was over 26 feet (8 meters) long. That is bigger than a 2.2-ton saltwater crocodile.

In 1961 three woodcutters were scared by a huge lizard. They guessed it was about 23 feet (7 meters) long. That is much bigger than the biggest Komodo dragon on record.

Frank Gordon was a scientist who studied **reptiles.** In 1979 he was out in the mountains of Australia. His car disturbed something that looked like a log. It **stirred** and then suddenly ran off. It was a lizard about 33 feet (10 meters) long. Could these lizards have been Megalania?

This Megalania skull proves this monster was real.

If the Megalania still exists, why have none been caught? Maybe it is because:

1   They keep out of sight.

2   They hunt at night.

3   They lie still and look like logs.

After all, Komodo dragons have only recently been discovered.

MYSTERY BEASTS OF THE MOUNTAINS

WHAT DOES THE YETI LOOK LIKE?

Everyone who has seen the yeti gives the same description:

* It has long, dark hair.
* It is like an ape with no tail.
* It walks upright like a man, but is much bigger.
* It has a strong, **vile** smell.

There may be a monster hiding in mountains around the world. It has many names. But whatever people call the hairy, ape-like creature, climbers keep reporting that it really is out there.

THE YETI

The mountains around Mount Everest are **bleak** and empty. Unless you believe the stories that say something lives there. We call the mountain monster the **Abominable** Snowman. Local people of Tibet and Nepal call him "*yah-teh*," or *yeti*. *Yeti* means "that thing of the mountains."

Many attempts have been made to find a yeti. It is like looking for a needle in a haystack. This is a **vast** wild country. The land is rocky, icy, and very high up. It is a very **hostile** environment.

habitat   natural home or environment
hostile   unfriendly or against you

A LUCKY ESCAPE

In 1974 a girl was alone in the mountains looking after her **yaks.** Suddenly she heard a loud grunt, and a yeti came running toward her. She tried to run, but the yeti grabbed her. There was nothing she could do but scream. Luckily the yeti dropped her in a stream and grabbed one of the yaks. It seemed to be in a rage. It easily killed the yak with its bare hands. The girl ran home in terror. The police found large footprints in the snow, but no yeti was to be seen. The yeti seems to be very good at escaping and hiding.

This hand is thought to have come from a yeti skeleton. It is kept in a **monastery** at the foot of Mount Everest in Nepal.

PROOF?

Here is some **evidence** that the yeti exists:

- Sightings over hundreds of years.
- Fuzzy photos of an ape-like creature.
- Huge footprints in the snow.
- Yaks have been killed and their bodies left half-eaten.
- Tests on hair match no known animal.

Were these huge footprints made by a yeti? >>

monastery   place where a group of monks live
yak   long-haired mountain ox

BIGFOOT FACTS

What makes us so sure there is really a Bigfoot out there? Perhaps because:

- People have reported seeing hairy, humanlike beasts in the wilderness in North America for over 400 years.
- Reports keep coming in from **reliable** people who are convinced they have seen it.
- For over 70 years, people have found sets of large human-shaped tracks in **remote** areas.

These plaster casts were taken of huge footprints found in mud. **>>**

MYSTERY APE-HUMAN

The hills and forests of North America may hide the mountain monster, too.

Native Americans have told stories of "the big hairy man" for hundreds of years. Some call it Sasquatch and others call it Bigfoot.

Some Native American tribes see Bigfoot as an older brother who keeps a friendly eye on them. They say it knows when people go looking for it, so it hides in the mountains. Not many people have been able to film Bigfoot. But it may not be long before someone finds real proof, one way or the other. Is Bigfoot real, or a big **hoax**?

hoax   untrue story made up for a joke

MANY SIGHTINGS

Reports say that Bigfoot can have black, red, or gray hair. Some people say it is shy and harmless, but others say it is **hostile.**

Here a man describes what he saw in Kentucky in 2003. He was driving on Highway 92, near the town of Pine Knot:

"I saw something ahead at the side of the road. Maybe it was a deer, so I slowed down. As I got close, I was shocked. It was over 6.5 feet (2 meters) tall and covered in gray hair. It looked at me with big red eyes. It seemed to be angry. I was scared to death and drove off fast."

FAMOUS FILM

Roger Patterson shot a famous film in 1967. He was on a horse when he came across Bigfoot. Or so he said. Some people think it is a hoax, but others think it is real. It is one of the only films of Bigfoot in all these years.

Shots from Roger Patterson's film.

reliable   sensible and trustworthy

TERROR

Even fierce dogs are said to tremble if a Yowie is near. Many campers have seen a hairy visitor at night raiding garbage cans. It eats anything, even kangaroos! Then it staggers off with a terrifying cry and that **vile** smell.

YOWIE AND ALMA

The Australian **Aborigines** have told stories for thousands of years. One of the stories is about a hairy "evil spirit" named Yowie that lived in the forests and hills. But is this just **folklore,** or is Yowie alive and well today? Could Yowie be Australia's version of Bigfoot?

Over the last hundred years, many people in Australia have reported Yowie sightings. The creature is said to be about 7.5 feet (2.3 meters) tall, with long brown hair. It makes a grunting noise and its **stench** is worse than rotten eggs. Stories say that Yowie's eyes glow yellow in the moonlight.

Yowies are thought to have enormous feet and hands. **‹‹**

Aborigine   person of one of the native cultures of Australia

TALL BEAST OR A TALL STORY?

Yeti, Bigfoot, and Yowie all sound like similar monsters. All the other ape-humans from around the world sound alike, too. They are all a similar size, shape, and smell, and live in the same kinds of places. Could they all be just a **hoax**?

Alma is another member of the family. It lives in the forests and hills of Russia and China. Alma's fur is white up in the mountains, but brown in the forests.

In 1997 many Alma footprints were studied in China. Each print was 14 inches (36 centimeters) long. Experts said a creature of over 440 pounds (200 kilograms) and at least 6.5 feet (2 meters) tall must have made them.

Yowie and Alma can survive the coldest of winters thanks to their thick, wooly coats. A snow drift is no match for them.

A sign in Washington state warns of Bigfoot crossing the road.

stench   foul smell
vile   really disgusting

23

MONSTERS OF THE SKY

GIANT BIRD OF THUNDER

Thunderbirds that carry humans away are part of Native American **folklore.** The birds have been described as having wingspans of over 33 feet (10 meters), hooked **talons,** and razor-sharp beaks.

Are there really monster birds up in the sky that could carry off a human? It sounds like **fantasy,** but maybe it could happen.

MONSTER BIRDS

Large eagles have been known to carry away baby deer that weigh up to 33 pounds (15 kilograms). Some are believed to snatch human babies. In 1868 a teacher in Missouri watched in horror as an eagle grabbed an eight-year-old boy from the school playground. It lifted him high into the air and dropped him to his death.

If an eagle could do this, what about a monster bird twice the size? Such birds once flew in parts of the world. According to some people, they still do.

Could a giant eagle grab a child with its sharp talons? >>

The Native Americans of Illinois call the thunderbird a Piasa Monster Bird. The bird has been part of folklore for hundreds of years, as shown on this magazine cover. <<

FATE MAGAZINE

TRUE STORIES OF THE STRANGE AND THE UNKNOWN

March 1954   35¢

MONSTER ON THE ROCK

THE COUPLE WHO LIVED
TELEPHONE BETWEEN

WEIRD WORDS   **fantasy**   from the world of dreams and imagination
talons   claws of a bird of prey

ON THE WINGS OF STORMS

Any bird with a 20-foot (6-meter) wingspan would need strong **thermal air currents** to keep it in the sky. A moving storm sucks up air into the clouds, creating these currents. A huge bird is said to arrive when these storms break out. Its name is the thunderbird. Many reports say such a bird has been spotted in Illinois.

In 1977 two giant birds appeared in the sky above Lawndale, Illinois. One of them grabbed ten-year-old Marlon Lowe. His mother screamed as the bird lifted him into the air. He hit the bird, and it dropped him nearby before flying off. He was left shocked and scratched. Experts say no known American bird would do this.

WINGED MONSTER IN THE HUACHUCA DESERT

In 1890 a cowboy named Jimmy Bradshaw said he was attacked by a thunderbird as he rode in the desert. He shot at it many times before it fell from the sky. "This was like no other bird I ever saw. It must have been the size of a horse," he said.

thermal air currents rising gusts of warm air

One **species** of this reptile was:

- the largest flying creature of all time;
- like a **vulture** that fed on dinosaur bodies;
- bigger than a light aircraft.

The first **fossils** of this giant were found in 1972 in Texas.

FLYING MONSTER

In the days when **dinosaurs** lived, huge beasts also swept across the sky. One was like a giant hangglider that drifted on air currents. It was called a pterosaur (*TERA-sore*), and its wingspan was over 39 feet (12 meters). That is about the same as a small airplane! Like all flying **reptiles,** it became **extinct.** At least we think it did.

EVERYTHING IS BIG IN TEXAS!

In 1976 a police patrol car was driving through Brownsville, Texas, early in the morning. It was just getting light outside. The two police officers suddenly looked up at a huge shadow in the sky. They could not believe their eyes. They could only shout into the radio.

No one knows for sure what color a pterosaur really was, but models have been made.

Aztec   ancient Native American civilization
species   type of living thing

OUT OF THIS WORLD

A short time later, a man in the same town heard thumping outside his home. When he looked out the window, he saw an enormous bird in his yard. "It's like a bird, but it's not a bird," he said. "That animal is not from this world."

MORE SIGHTINGS

More people said they had seen the "flying monster." Some teachers told of a large flying beast that dived at their cars as they drove to work. One of them rushed to the library and found a name for the animal: a pterosaur.

Things turned quiet after that. The skies of Texas returned to normal. Until next time . . .

SURPRISE OF THE CIVIL WAR

U.S. soldiers had a shock 130 years ago. A report tells how they shot down three pterodactyls. The pterodactyl is the pterosaur's cousin. It was all kept a secret because no other details were known. Was it just a **hoax**? It is a real mystery.

Aztecs worshiped a flying **serpent**. Did this **legend** come from real sightings of pterodactyls, which are also reptiles with wings? «

vulture   large bird that feeds on dead bodies

27

THE HUGE BIRD

The Roc was a giant bird in **myths,** with feathers as big as palm leaves. It could carry an elephant in its claws and drop it from a great height. Some say it once lived on the island of Madagascar, in the Indian Ocean.

GIANT VULTURE

The largest bird that ever lived was a teratorn. It was as heavy as a human, but it could still fly because of its huge wings. It would **soar** like a **condor,** but it was far bigger. This giant **vulture** is said to have died out in the last Ice Age. But did it?

ALIVE IN ALASKA?

At the end of 2002, many people in Alaska reported seeing a strange bird. It was huge and looked nothing like an ordinary bird. They said it could not be one of the local sea birds. It was as big as a light aircraft. People said it looked like something out of the movie *Jurassic Park.*

There are fewer than 100 California condors left in the wild. ❯❯

The Roc could carry off large animals like horses.

WEIRD WORDS   condor   very large vulture that lives in North and South America

IS IT A BIRD, IS IT A PLANE, IS IT A TERATORN?

The giant bird amazed people in the town of Togiak, Alaska. A pilot who lived there laughed when he heard the reports, thinking it must be a joke. But then he saw the bird just 985 feet (300 meters) away while he was flying his plane. "He's huge, he's really, really big," he said. "You wouldn't want to have your children out."

STILL A MYSTERY

The U.S. Fish and Wildlife Service said there had been sightings over the past year of Steller's sea eagles in Alaska. These eagles are fish-eating birds that can have a wingspan of 6.5 to 10 feet (2 to 3 meters). Even so, the mystery has not been solved.

The moa could not fly. >>

THE EXTINCT GIANT MOA

The giant moa was one of the biggest birds ever known. It was over 10 feet (3 meters) tall and weighed 550 pounds (250 kilograms). In 1994 three hikers in New Zealand said they saw a live moa. It was reported around the world.

MONSTERS OF THE LAKE

FACT OR FICTION?

Some people say the Loch Ness Monster is nonsense. It is all made up to boost the tourist trade in Scotland. They say it is just a giant eel, a seal, or a big fish. They say the photos are a **hoax** or just show a log, a wave, or an otter.

Thousands of lakes with deep, murky water hide many secrets. Sometimes something stirs in the water . . . something huge.

THE LOCH NESS MONSTER

For over 1,000 years, the mystery deep in Scotland's **Loch** Ness has brought monster hunters searching for "Nessie." A road was made around the loch about 70 years ago. Since then, many more people have reported seeing the Loch Ness Monster.

FILM STAR?

It was then that famous monster photos began to appear. The world was amazed and wanted to know more about the creature with humps, a long tail, and a head like a snake. The photo shown on this page turned out to be a fake, but the search still continues.

HUNDREDS OF REPORTS

Many people say they have seen a large head rise out of the loch. Some people say they have seen "a huge beast with flippers" on the bank. There could be a whole family of mysterious creatures **lurking** in the loch.

No otter has a neck this long!

30   **WEIRD WORDS**

loch   Scottish lake
lurk   to wait around, ready to strike

THE HUNT GOES ON

One night a scientist in a boat detected something with **sonar**. He said, "Rowing across that pitch-black water and knowing there was a very large animal just below my boat was frightening."

Scientists have used minisubmarines, too. Now it is possible to try to spy on Nessie using a webcam. How long will it be now before Nessie appears live on-screen?

Fast fact

Go to www.lochness.co.uk/livecam and see if you can find the Loch Ness Monster on the live webcam.

Loch Ness is 24 miles (39 km) long and 1 miles (2 km) wide. In places it is deep enough to hide a 40-story building.

SHADOWS BELOW

In 1987 many boats scanned Loch Ness in the search for the monster. The sonar scans showed large shapes moving deep in the loch. They may have been huge fish. Or were they a family of monsters?

This is a sonar image taken in Loch Ness. The yellow mark shows that there is something big in the water.

A monster has been reported in Lake Kos in Russia. People claim it is 49 feet (15 meters) long with a head 6.5 feet (2 meters) long by 3 feet (1 meter) wide. In 1977, Moscow Radio reported that "**extinct**" creatures may really have **survived**. "Unknown creatures might still exist," it said.

FAMILY

More than 250 of the world's lakes and rivers are reported to have some sort of strange beast. Some of these are in Scotland. Nessie is not alone.

LEFT OVER AFTER MILLIONS OF YEARS?

People first learned about **dinosaurs** in 1841. Before then, no one knew about "water dinosaurs." Yet for hundreds of years, people described how Nessie looked. They told stories of a creature just like what we now know to be a **plesiosaur**. This was a large **reptile** with a neck up to 16 feet (5 meters) long. It had four large flippers, like wings to move it through water, and many teeth.

plesiosaur   large, extinct marine animal with paddlelike flippers and a long neck

DOUBTS

Could all of the lake monsters that have been reported really be plesiosaurs? Or could all the sightings over hundreds of years just be jokes? Is there more to the stories than that? There are still many questions. Scientists are still waiting for firm proof.

HOW TO GET RICH

A student took a video of what he said was a monster in Lake Van in Turkey. The creature was slimy and black and had horns on its head. But fuzzy film does not prove much. People have tried to make millions of dollars from fake films. The world still waits for a clear film showing a real lake monster.

A SWEDISH SECOND COUSIN

Lake Storsjön in Sweden is famous, like Loch Ness. A large creature was first spotted there 350 years ago. Since 1987 there have been 400 reports of the 20-foot- (6-meter-) long beast. It is gray-brown on top with a yellow belly.

Sometimes playful seals can fool anyone!

OGOPOGO

There is supposed to be a monster named Ogopogo in Lake Okanagan in British Columbia, Canada. **Radar** has yet to find it once and for all. Perhaps the moving shadows are just a very large sturgeon fish. After all, sturgeon can grow up to 26 feet (8 meters) long.

AMERICAN LAKES

Canada and the United States are full of deep, dark lakes. Perhaps lakes are full of deep, dark monsters.

CHAMP

Lake Champlain borders New York and Vermont. It is over 100 miles (160 kilometers) long. As far back as 1609, people saw strange things in the water. In 1883 the Sheriff of Clinton County, New York said he saw a fat snake about 30 feet (10 meters) long in the lake. Then, sailors saw a large shape leave the water and crawl up the beach.

The monster is named Champ, and there is only one photo of it. It looks like a **plesiosaur.** Other people have reported seeing it more recently.

This royal sturgeon was caught in the English Channel in 1947. It weighed over 400 pounds (180 kilograms)— as much as a full-grown lion.

radar   using radio waves to find and track objects

TESSIE

Lake Tahoe, bordering California and Nevada, is home to "Tessie," a dark snake-like creature over 65 feet (20 meters) long. There is a film of something big swimming in the lake, but scientists have not been able to find it. In the 1800s, the Washoe Native Americans told stories of such a beast living in the lake. Every year more Tessie sightings are reported.

Manipogo might be a huge, fierce fish like this.

No one can agree what Champ looks like. These are two possibilities.

MANIPOGO

There is another monster named Manipogo. It is said to live in Canada's Lake Manitoba. There have been reports of a huge snake-like creature in the lake since 1908. There is still no real proof—just a photo of a shape. That could be almost anything.

A REAL MIX

In 1848 a bunyip was seen with a round head, long neck, and body like an ox. Others said it was half horse and half crocodile. It was bigger than an elephant, with eyes like fire and tusks like a walrus.

THE BUNYIP

Australian **Aboriginies** told tales of these weird creatures. Bunyips are are supposed to **lurk** in swamps, riverbeds, and waterholes. The name *bunyip* means "devil." They come out at night with **blood-curdling** cries. They kill any animal or human that dares to come near it. However, the bunyip's favorite **prey** is supposed to be women and children. Their tender flesh is just right, and any shape or size will do. The bunyip is not choosy.

ALL SORTS

It seems that bunyips come in all shapes and sizes. They can have long tails or necks, wings, claws, horns, trunks, fur, **scales,** fins, and feathers. They all kill their prey the same way—by hugging it to death!

A large walrus might look like a bunyip.

blood-curdling   horrifying
culture   customs and traditions of a country

TASMANIA

In 1913 Oscar Davies saw a bunyip in Tasmania. He reported that the creature was about 17 feet (5 meters) long and 4 feet (1.2 meters) high, with a small head and thick neck. It had shiny brown fur, four legs, and ran fast. It left footprints that were about 9 inches (22 centimeters) across. That does not sound like an average walrus.

LONG BLACK HAIR

Back in 1872 a man said he saw a bunyip in a **lagoon** at Wagga Wagga in Australia. He said it looked like "a dog with really long black hair all over its body." If a woman or child disappeared, everyone used to fear the worst. Had a bunyip struck again? The good news is that there have not been many sightings lately.

JUST MYTH?

Whatever the bunyip really is, it has become a star of children's stories. It is now part of the **culture** in Australia. After looking at possible bunyip bones, however, many Australians are sure that the bunyip is just a **myth**.

Australian Aborigines traditionally hunted in lagoons and waterholes. Did they spot bunyips in the water? »

lagoon   saltwater lake by a sea or ocean
prey   victim to be killed and eaten

MONSTERS OF THE SEAS

MONSTER OF THE WAVES

A bishop from Norway was on his way to Greenland in 1734. A huge sea serpent raised its head from the ocean—as high as the ship's mast. When it fell back into the sea, its tail was said to be longer than the ship itself.

There were no cameras in the 1700s, so people made carvings of the monsters they claimed to have seen. ∨∨

Sailors through the ages have told scary tales about sea **serpents.** Maybe on long voyages they had nothing better to do than make up **far-fetched** stories. Unless, of course, the stories were true.

HMS *DAEDALUS*

In 1848 seven sailors aboard the ship *Daedalus* saw a strange creature in the ocean as they sailed near Cape Town in South Africa. The captain said it was a 45-foot- (14-meter-) long sea serpent. It swam beside the ship for about 20 minutes. The monster's head was over 3 feet (1 meter) out of the water. Its jaws were big enough to eat a man in one gulp. Everyone on board the ship was terrified.

The frilled shark is one of the strangest-looking sea creatures. Its long, thin body and large, gaping mouth make it very serpent-like. ∧∧

WEIRD WORDS   far-fetched   hard to believe

THE SEA SERPENT OF GLOUCESTER

For over 300 years, hundreds of people have told stories about the sea serpent of Gloucester port in Massachusetts. In 1817 **shipmaster** Allen wrote about the sea serpent:

"His head was like a rattlesnake's, but as large as the head of a horse. He slowly moved on the surface of the water in circles."

SHOT

Another sailor shot at the serpent and said: *"I took good aim at his head. I must have hit him. He turned toward me after I had fired, and I thought he was coming at us. But he sank down and went directly under our boat."*

LOOK-ALIKE

The oarfish is an eel-like animal that can be over 26 feet (8 meters) long—maybe even double this size. It is silver with bright red spikes running down its back. Two men killed a giant one near Bermuda in 1860. They thought it was a sea serpent.

Has an oarfish like this been mistaken for a monster?

shipmaster   guard in charge of the harbor

TYPES OF SEA MONSTERS REPORTED

1 Merhorse: large eyes, smooth skin, and a mane.

2 Multi-humped: whale-like with several humps.

3 Long-necked: small head and four flippers.

4 Super eel: giant eel-like fish, no limbs.

5 Yellow belly: tadpole-shaped, yellow with a black stripe.

ATLANTIC MONSTER

You may see a sea monster named Chessie where the Chester River meets the ocean near Baltimore, Maryland. Every so often a ripple moves across calm water. A black creature 33 feet (10 meters) long pops its head up. A **witness** once said, "The eye looked like a serpent's. It didn't look like a fish."

Sometimes groups of people see Chessie. In 1980, 25 people in four boats saw Chessie at the same time. In 1982 Robert Frew filmed a long, dark creature swimming in Chesapeake Bay, along the east coast of the United States. It was about 33 feet (10 meters) long with a humped back. Then it dived under some swimmers. They quickly swam to shore.

This map shows where sea monsters have been spotted in the United States.

Key to map
- Caddy
- Chessie
- Port Gloucester sea serpent

Seattle

N
W   E
S

0   500 miles

0   700 kilometers

• Los Angeles

United States

Chicago •

Boston •
New York •
Washington D.C.

Atlantic Ocean

Pacific Ocean

Gulf of Mexico

witness   someone who is there when something happens

PACIFIC MONSTER

Caddy is a sea monster that is supposed to live off the northwest coast of North America. People say that it has been popping up for over 1,000 years. They also say that:

- It is between 16 and 50 ft (5 and 15 m) long.
- Its body is snake-like, with a neck of 13 ft (4 m).
- Its head is said to be like that of a sheep, horse, giraffe, or camel.
- It has a pair of front flippers.
- Its tail is spiky.
- It can swim very fast.

People still say they see it around Vancouver Island in Canada. But what is it? Caddy remains a mystery.

QUESTIONS

What is Caddy? No one really knows. It could be a sea **dinosaur** from long ago. Maybe it is a type of whale we do not know about. The coast of North America is **remote** and borders one of the deepest underwater trenches in the world. Who knows what might hide there?

Anacondas live in the tropical rain forests of South America. They can grow up to 20 feet (6 meters) long. They like to eat deer, sheep, and dogs. Could they be a distant relative of these gigantic sea monsters? **«**

GIANT SQUID

Giant squid live deep in the ocean. These huge creatures are hardly ever seen, so we still know very little about them. Sometimes a dead giant squid is washed up onto a beach.

A giant squid can be as big as two buses. Its eyes are 20 inches (0.5 meter) across—the largest eyes in the world.

In 2003 a giant squid was caught in the Antarctic. It was the first time Dr. O'Shea had seen its five pairs of long arms with suckers and hooks. "It has to be one of the most frightening **predators** out there," he said.

The giant squid can kill whales, so a human would just be a snack.

Giant squid sometimes wash up onto beaches.

THE SS *TRESCO*

In 1903 the SS *Tresco* was sailing off the North Carolina coast. A sailor wrote:

"I saw something with a 100-foot (30-meter) body. The head was the size of a human. Our ship was in danger of tipping over if it tried to clamber aboard."

predator   animal that hunts and eats other animals

GIANT OCTOPUS

A cousin of the squid is the octopus, but this monster has eight arms. It lives on the ocean floor, up to several miles deep. Octopuses come in a range of sizes, but the question is, "How big can they get?"

Some sailors believe a giant octopus exists. It could weigh more than 10 tons and measure 100 feet (30 meters) across. That is a giant! An octopus half this size was found dead in 1896 on a Florida beach. Even this was a monster as big as a house.

The giant octopus may be the creature behind the kraken, which appears in Norwegian **myths.** Stories tell how the dreaded kraken could sink a ship and eat all the crew.

MYSTERY MONSTER

In 1964 Robert Serrec was on vacation in Australia. In shallow water off the coast, he saw a tadpole-like creature about 82 feet (25 meters) long. It seemed to have a wound on its back. He took pictures of the creature before it swam off. It was not seen again.

This is one of Robert Serrec's photos of a giant tadpole-like creature.

The harmless basking shark is often mistaken for a sea monster. It is one of the largest fish in the ocean. It can be over 39 feet (12 meters) long.

MYSTERIES OF THE FOREST

DEEP AND MYSTERIOUS

The Congo is a **vast** area. The thick forests have not changed for thousands of years. They could still hide animals we have never seen. In 1959 a pilot looked down on a huge snake over 49 feet (15 meters) long. Its huge head looked as if it was from another world.

There are secrets hiding deep in the swamps, jungles, and underground caves of Africa. One secret is in a large country called the Democratic Republic of Congo. People here have seen signs of a monster for over 200 years. Few people go deep into the dark, **waterlogged** forests. They call the monster *Mokele-mbembe*. It means "the one who stops the river."

Local people believe the monster is **sacred.** They say a tribe once killed a *Mokele-mbembe*. Many ate its meat and died, so perhaps the beast has a **curse.** Now everyone keeps well away from the monster's thick swamp.

What monsters **lurk** in the swamps of the Congo? >>

bulky   of stocky build, large and awkward
pillar   solid column that helps support a building

BAD TEMPER

The mystery beast has a long neck and short legs. It is bigger than an elephant. It is said to have smooth, brown skin and to spend a lot of time in water. Although this creature does not eat meat, it will attack humans or hippos. The monster seems to be very moody. It does not like to be disturbed. It is said that *Mokele-mbembe* will flip over boats. It then kills people by hitting them with its tail. Hippos stay away from these monsters.

LIVING DINOSAUR?

Big footprints with three claws have been found around the swamps. Some scientists think there may be a type of **dinosaur** here called a sauropod. But so far there is no real proof.

SAUROPOD DINOSAURS

These were plant-eating **reptiles.** They had small heads and little brains. Their bodies were **bulky,** with four **pillar-like** legs. They had long necks and tails. Dinosaurs were the largest animals on the earth. Some sauropods may have been 115 feet (35 meters) long and weighed more than 100 tons!

Lake Tele and Likoula Swamp in Africa may hide a creature only seen by a few people.

sacred   very special or holy
waterlogged   flooded with water

45

FAMILY

The tree sloth lives in the Amazon rain forest. It hangs from trees and moves very slowly from branch to branch. It is the nearest living relative of the giant ground sloth. However, a tree sloth is tiny when compared with its huge **extinct** cousin.

THE AMAZON MONSTER

Even today, we still do not know all the creatures that live on our planet. Many miles of thick jungle can still hide big beasts. The Amazon rain forest is among the largest in the world. There may be monsters hiding deep inside.

One such beast has a strange name as well as a strange smell. It is the mapinguari, a giant ground sloth. Tree sloths are hairy ape-like creatures that move very slowly in trees. But giant ground sloths were different. They once roamed over all North and South America. For some reason they died out a few thousand years ago. But maybe not *all* of them died.

The tree sloth is only about 28 inches (70 centimeters) tall. It spends most of its life upside-down in trees.

forester   someone who plants and manages forests

A BAD SMELL

This rare animal is said to have stood several meters tall. It had long red-brown hair. Over 50 people say they have seen a mapinguari in the last 30 years. One **witness** was Mário de Souza. He came across a giant sloth along a river in Brazil in 1975. He said, "The horrible smell hit me and made me dizzy. I was not right for two months."

This Cambodian stamp shows the mapinguari.

Some Brazilian **foresters** swear they have seen mapinguari kill men by twisting off their heads and cracking open their skulls. This may seem **far-fetched,** but why would these foresters lie?

EXTINCT?

Giant ground sloths lived a few thousand years ago in North and South America. One fossil is 20 feet (6 meters) high, like an elephant that could stand on two legs. It was a megatherium. Could the mystery beast in the Amazon be another megatherium?

This megatherium skeleton is displayed at the Natural History Museum in London.

47

MONSTER OF SOUTH AMERICA

In 1999 Brazil's *Corriero* newspaper reported that eight goats and three sheep were found dead with wounds to the neck. Other **witnesses** claimed to have seen an animal that can leap with strong, monkey-like legs. It is said to attack animals and humans.

CHUPACABRA

Imagine a vampire mixed with Bigfoot. This monster could be the chupacabra from the South American rain forest. It seems to visit the United States, too.

A REPORT FROM 2002

A boy told how he met a chupacabra in Salt Lake City, Utah. "We got to my friend's farm and turned on the porch lights. There was growling behind us and I saw a monkey-like creature with no tail and glowing eyes. It ran off into the woods. My friend followed, but it chased him out again. Later my friend found his two goats dead. They were drained of blood, with bite marks in their necks. His dog disappeared and was never found."

Goats seem to be the chupacabra's favorite food.

STRANGE

In 1995 there were ten reports of chupacabra attacks on goats in Puerto Rico. Newspapers described it as a little monster with bulging red eyes, fangs, and a long, darting tongue. Its name means "goat-sucker," since it drinks the blood of goats and sheep. It is said to be the size and shape of a baboon.

This creature is a puzzle. Can it really exist? Some reports seem **far-fetched,** yet the stories have been told for over 50 years. Hundreds of these tales come from Brazil and Chile in South America. But lately the monster has been reported across the United States, too. Perhaps it is on the **prowl.**

CAN IT BE EXPLAINED?

Many reports say a chupacabra:

* is a gray-brown ape-like creature;

* has three horns on its head;

* hops like a kangaroo and is able to leap or "fly";

* feeds on farm animals like a vampire.

The Amazon rain forest covers an area half the size of the United States. That is big enough to hide more than a few secrets.

49

LAND OF THE GIANTS

THE FIRST OF ITS KIND

The Lost World was the first story about dinosaurs. It was about a man searching the jungle for a hidden **plateau**. He had heard that the plateau was locked in the past. It was a lost world with monsters from another age. What he found in this world has sparked our imaginations ever since.

Monsters once ruled the earth. Now we think humans do. But maybe there really are a few monsters still **lurking** out there. After all, people often say they see them. Is it just their minds playing tricks? Is it all just for fun? Or do some people want to believe in monsters so much that they make themselves see them? Maybe someone will soon prove that one of these mysterious creatures exists.

We are still finding out about huge **dinosaurs** that lived millions of years ago. The first story about them was written in 1912 by Arthur Conan Doyle. It was called *The Lost World*.

A scene from *The Lost World* in which the explorers' dinner is stolen by a pterodactyl. **》》**

clone   to breed an exact copy of a creature using its DNA

SCIENCE FACT OR FICTION?

Ever since *The Lost World* came out, books and movies have made us worry. What if dinosaurs are still alive? What if they come back?

Maybe it could happen. After all, scientists keep finding bodies of **extinct** creatures in ice or in tar pits. They are taken to laboratories and their cells are studied. One day scientists hope to make new life from what they find in these cells. They are already trying to **clone** a baby mammoth. Perhaps it is just a matter of time before extinct monsters walk again.

Maybe the mysterious monsters of the past are already on their way back . . . .

The dinosaurs in today's movies look like the real thing.

JURASSIC PARK AND ANOTHER LOST WORLD

In 1990 Michael Crichton wrote *Jurassic Park*. It is about theme-park dinosaurs that begin to attack humans. This book made dinosaur stories popular again.

His next book had a familiar title—the same as one 83 years before. It was *The Lost World*. Once more, monsters were fighting back!

plateau   piece of land that is raised up higher than the land around it. It is similar to a mountain with a flat top.

FIND OUT MORE

MONSTER WEBSITES

DINORAMA

Excellent guide to dinosaurs with the latest dinosaur news. **nationalgeographic. com/dinorama**

BIGFOOT FIELD RESEARCHERS ORGANIZATION

A website that reports Bigfoot sightings. The site also has pictures and other information on Bigfoot. **bfro.net**

BOOKS

Matsen, Bradford. *Incredible Hunt for the Giant Squid*. Berkeley Heights, NJ: Enslow, 2003.

Wallace, Holly. *Mystery of the Abominable Snowman*. Chicago: Heinemann, 1999.

Wallace, Holly. *Mystery of the Loch Ness Monster*. Chicago: Heinemann, 1999.

WORLD WIDE WEB

If you want to find out more about monsters, you can search the Internet using keywords such as these:

- monster + Frankenstein
- "Komodo Dragon"
- Megalania + skull
- vampires + [name of a country]
- "Loch Ness Monster"

You can also find your own keywords by using headings or words from this book. Use the search tips opposite to help you find the most useful websites.

SEARCH TIPS

There are billions of pages on the Internet, so it can be difficult to find exactly what you are looking for. If you just type in "monster" on a search engine such as Google, you will get a list of fifteen million web pages. These search skills will help you find useful websites more quickly:

- Know exactly what you want to find out.
- Use simple keywords, not whole sentences.
- Use two to six keywords in a search.
- Be precise—only use names of people, places, or things.
- If you want to find words that go together, put quote marks around them.
- Use the "+" sign to add certain words—for example typing "monster + games" into the search box will help you find web pages with games related to monsters.

SEARCH ENGINE

A search engine looks through the entire Web and lists all the sites that match the words in the search box. The best matches are at the top of the list, on the first page. Try **google.com**.

SEARCH DIRECTORY

A search directory is like a library of websites. You can search by keyword or subject and browse through the different sites as you would look through books on a shelf. A good example is **yahooligans.com**.

GLOSSARY

abominable   terrible, disgusting
Aborigine   person of one of the native cultures of Australia
ambush   surprise attack
ancient   from a past age long ago
Aztec ancient Native American civilization
bleak   barren, cold, and windy
blood-curdling horrifying
boar   large wild pig
bulky   of stocky build, large and awkward
business   trade for making money
clone   to breed an exact copy of a creature using the genetic information found in its cells
condor   very large vulture that lives in North and South America
culture   customs and traditions of a country
curse   strange power that brings harm to some people
Dark Ages   over 1,000 years ago, when people knew little about the world or science
dinosaur   huge reptiles from prehistoric times. They are now extinct.
evidence   information that can help prove if something is true or false

extinct   died out, never to return
fantasy   from the world of dreams and imagination
far-fetched   hard to believe
fiction   made-up story from the imagination
folklore   old beliefs, myths, and stories
forester   someone who plants and manages forests
fossils   ancient remains of animal bones and teeth
glinted   sparkled with light
hoax   untrue story or prank. Created to fool people.
hostile   unfriendly or against you
lagoon   saltwater lake by the ocean
legend   story from long ago that may be partly true
loch   Scottish lake
lurking   waiting around, ready to strike
maiden   young, unmarried woman
mammal   animal that has hair and nurses its young. Humans are mammals.
monastery   where a group of monks lives
myth   made-up tale, told over many years

54

outback wild country, with desert, scrubland, and swamps. It usually refers to part of Australia.

pillar solid column that helps support a building

plateau piece of land that is raised up higher than the land around it. It is similar to a mountain with a flat top.

plesiosaur large marine animal with paddle-like flippers and a long neck

predator animal that hunts and eats other animals

prey to hunt down to kill. Also, a victim to be killed and eaten.

rabies disease caught from the bite of an infected animal

radar using radio waves to find and track objects

reliable sensible and trustworthy

remote far away from people

reptiles cold-blooded animals that lay eggs, such as snakes and lizards

sacred very special or holy

saliva mouth juices, spit

scales small bony plates that protect the skin. They are found on fish and reptiles.

serpent large snake

shipmaster guard in charge of the harbor

slay to kill

soar to fly high and glide in the sky

sonar using sound waves to detect objects underwater

species type of living thing

stake stick or post sharpened at one end

stench disgusting smell

stirred started to move after being asleep or still for some time

survive stay alive despite dangers

talons claws of a bird of prey

thermal air currents rising gusts or drafts of warm air

trench long, narrow, deep ditch or valley on the ocean floor

triumph success and victory

vast very large area

vile really disgusting

vulture large bird that feeds on dead bodies

waterlogged flooded with water

witness someone who is there when something happens

yak long-haired mountain ox

INDEX